A Field Guide to

Exmoor's Early Iron Industry

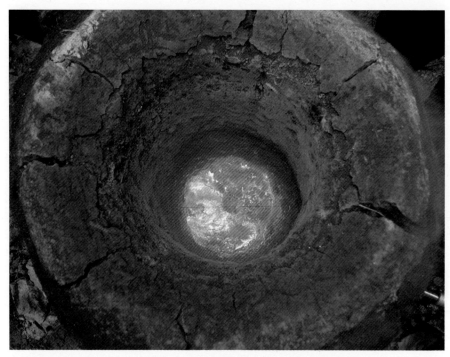

View from above of the interior of an experimental furnace during smelting
(© Exmoor Iron Project).

Introduction

Exmoor has been shaped by natural agencies such as geology, climate, vegetation and wildlife. Taken together these factors contribute to the sublime backdrop, but it is the activities of people over the last 8000 years which have shaped the landscape that we see today. Chiefly, this has been the result of farming which has created the complex and intricate patterns of hedged fields. The moorlands are a direct result of people clearing the forests and even the woodlands themselves are the product of hundreds of years of management. Perhaps the most unexpected influence, though, is industry and in particular mineral extraction.

Mineral resources have been exploited on Exmoor for thousands of years and much of what we know about these industries is derived from historical records from the 19th century. Exmoor was a source of silver, lead and copper at least as far back as the medieval period, whilst lime and slate have been produced in more recent centuries. All have left their mark, but iron ore was the most extensively exploited and was mined on a very large scale in the Brendon Hills in the 19th century.

This guide will focus on the production of iron before the Industrial Revolution; it will examine the span of time from the prehistoric to the medieval period. The evidence for this industry is almost entirely archaeological and takes the form of mine workings and deposits of iron smelting waste. These remains are still recognizable in many places across Exmoor and the Brendon Hills. Although sometimes subtle and unprepossessing, these sites form an integral part of the story of mineral exploitation in south-west England, historically one of the world's greatest mining provinces, in which the production of metals has been a major influence on cultural development. Exmoor's iron production sites are also extremely well-preserved and present a chance to examine how the character and technology of such activities has adapted to changing economic and social conditions over long periods of time. The early mining remains of the region have usually not been effaced by recent industrial extraction. Although 19th century mining occurred, most of it was focused on the Brendon Hills (with some efforts within the former Royal Forest of Exmoor). Elsewhere, the remoteness of the region limited attempts to open up iron mines to a number of largely unsuccessful trials.

Geology

The story of iron on Exmoor begins in the extreme, distant past; in the geological period known as the Devonian, which began around 395 million years ago. At this time, the area which was to become Exmoor was submerged in a shallow sea. Just to the north, in what is now Wales, lay a continental landmass, its coastline extending from southern Ireland, roughly along the line of the Bristol Channel to the Thames Estuary, while to the south, over the rest of Devon and Cornwall, the water deepened into an oceanic trough. Exmoor lay in relatively shallow coastal waters into which rivers running south off the northern landmass deposited the sediments which today form the shales, slates and sandstones that are the bones of the modern Exmoor landscape.

This situation continued for something like 50 million years with the water covering the Exmoor region gradually deepening as the sea advanced over the eroding continent to the north. Then, around 345 million years ago, the movement of tectonic plates to the south began to thrust the sea-floor sediments, now converted to rocks, upwards, folding them into a vast mountain range that probably rivalled the modern Himalayas in height. It was at this time that the story of iron on Exmoor began. Under the conditions of intense heat and pressure generated by the mountain-building episode, circulating fluids contained within the rocks were able to leach out and concentrate metal minerals, redepositing them in fractures, thus forming bodies of ore. Millions of years of erosion followed until, in the relatively recent past, these ore deposits were exposed at the surface as outcrops which could be discovered and exploited.

Exmoor has three main types of ore bodies, which include those dominated by lead and silver minerals which are concentrated in the vicinity of Combe Martin in the north-west, and those containing a mixture of copper and iron minerals located mainly along the southern fringes of Exmoor. However, most abundant are those containing predominantly iron minerals, which run in a broad belt, following the east-west trend of the geology, across the central and southern parts of Exmoor, extending into the Brendon Hills in the east.

The Archaeological Context

At Roman Lode, south of Simonsbath, recent research has revealed Early Bronze Age activity, close to a rich vein of iron ore. Whilst the meaning of this activity is unclear it may represent the earliest evidence of people interacting with Exmoor's iron deposits. At this time people constructed many of the monuments that are found across Exmoor today, such as round barrows and stone settings. The siting of these monuments suggest that people attached great significance to the landscape, and presumably the deposits of iron ore that outcropped in many places on Exmoor would also have featured in this relationship. Before they were mined these ore deposits would often have been obvious and unusual features: outcropping quartz and intensely red-stained rocks combined with

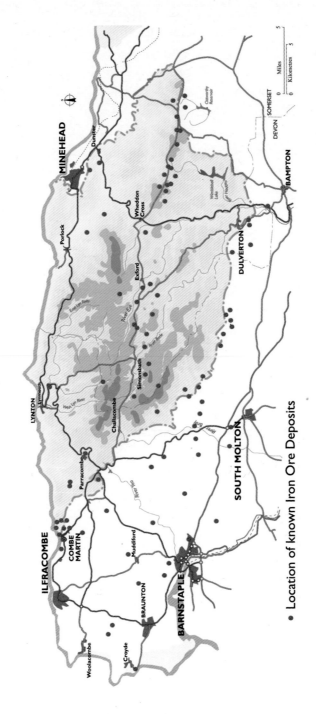

• Location of known Iron Ore Deposits

Map showing the locations of known iron deposits in the Exmoor region.

© Copyright Exmoor National Park 2010

vegetation changes would certainly have attracted the attention of local people.

The ensuing Middle Bronze Age saw people expanding their farming lifestyle by laying out field systems and settlements; the traces of which still survive in the landscape today. During this time, lasting around a thousand years from c.1500 BC, there is no evidence of human engagement with the iron resources of the region.

It is likely that the exploitation of Exmoor's iron deposits for metal began in the Iron Age during the last few centuries BC, but no firm evidence has yet come to light. There are shadowy hints of activity at Sherracombe Ford and Sindercombe Farm near Twitchen during the Iron Age. These take the form of radiocarbon dates spanning the late 1st century BC and the 1st century AD, but it is difficult to draw reliable conclusions about the beginnings of iron production on Exmoor from these.

Archaeologists date the beginning of the Roman Period to AD 43, the year of the Roman invasion of Britain under Emperor Claudius. According to the archaeological and palaeoenvironmental record, everyday life for the inhabitants of Exmoor continued largely unchanged. People continued to live mostly in round houses very similar to those of their ancestors and they probably farmed the landscape in much the same way. However, in other ways Roman rule brought significant changes. The people of the south-west were known to the Romans as the Dumnonii and, following the departure of the military garrison in the late 1st century, a self-governing province known as the Civitas Dumnoniorum was founded, based on the new town of Isca Dumnoniorum; modern Exeter. The growth of Romano-British culture also involved a significant increase in both the amount of iron used and the range of its applications. This, combined with the establishment of stable political conditions prompted, during the 2nd century AD, the first clear signs of iron production in the Exmoor region. This is in the form of smelting sites at Clatworthy Reservoir,

Sherracombe Ford and Brayford which, in combination, probably produced an overall total of several thousand tonnes of refined iron. During the 3rd century the character of iron production changed with smaller-scale operations, such as that at Blacklake Wood, becoming typical. The reasons for this change are difficult to discern, but one possibility is that the size of accessible markets was shrinking in the more unsettled political conditions at this time. In such an environment it would have been economically safer for those involved in iron production to put more resources into producing food.

From the beginning of the 5th century, the period known as the 'Dark Ages', there is virtually no evidence for iron production on Exmoor. By the 11th century four iron masters are recorded at North Molton (Domesday Book). The exact nature of their activity is unknown, but four iron workers seems a high number for a single settlement and it is possible they were smelters. The place names of North Molton and South Molton may relate to iron working activity in the vicinity, as 'moll' appears to originate in Ireland and mean 'heap', which may refer to the slag heaps from early iron workings.

By the medieval period, the centre of Exmoor is dominated by the Royal Forest. The remainder of the region was divided into manors held by other members of the nobility and the Church. Castles were constructed in three of these, at Bury near Dulverton, Holwell, near Parracombe and at Dunster. The modern settlement pattern of dispersed farmsteads and hamlets had started to emerge before the Norman Conquest and was established by the 11th century. However it is not until the early 14th century that tax returns confirm the detailed existence of the pattern. The known medieval iron smelting sites in the Barle Valley and at Oldrey are all small, presenting a very different picture to those of Roman date. The implication is that iron was being produced only for local needs and, given the brief occupation at these sites, perhaps only at times when metal could not be obtained easily from elsewhere.

The story of the exploitation of Exmoor's iron ore deposits is long; stretching back around 4000 years. The narrative is patchy like a novel with missing chapters, but we can determine in detail how iron was smelted during some periods, whilst in others the archaeological record is silent. Much more archaeological research is needed to enable some of the missing chapters to be written.

The Iron Production Process and its Archaeology

Iron production is the transformation of raw iron ore to usable metal. It is a complex and highly skilled process, but can be divided into several generic stages; mining, charcoal production, smelting and refining.

The basic raw materials needed to produce iron are:

- iron ore from which the metal is produced
- wood fuel in the form of charcoal.

The first stage of iron production is the mining of iron ore from the ground. Many mineral deposits rich in iron ore are present on Exmoor, distributed in a broad belt running from west to east across its centre and southern fringes. Commonly, these outcrop at the surface and so were readily identifiable and easily accessible to early miners who probably extracted the ore from small-scale, shallow opencast workings, which have left little trace today. The second basic raw material – charcoal - was required in larger volumes than iron ore, suggesting that iron working sites were located near to significant amounts of woodland. It is likely, given the amount consumed, that woodland management was needed to avoid deforestation.

The central stage of the iron production process is smelting which, most simply defined is the reduction of iron ore to metallic iron.

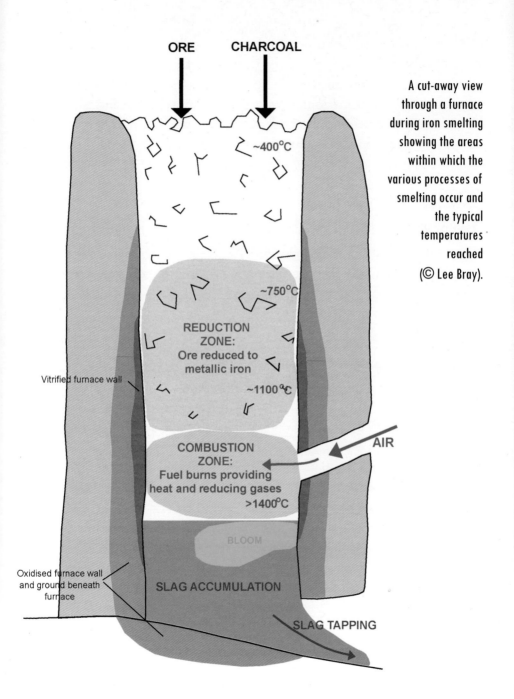

ORE CHARCOAL

~400°C

~750°C

REDUCTION
ZONE:
Ore reduced to
metallic iron

~1100°C

Vitrified furnace wall

COMBUSTION
ZONE:
Fuel burns providing
heat and reducing gases
>1400°C

AIR

BLOOM

Oxidised furnace wall
and ground beneath
furnace

SLAG ACCUMULATION

SLAG TAPPING

A cut-away view
through a furnace
during iron smelting
showing the areas
within which the
various processes of
smelting occur and
the typical
temperatures
reached
(© Lee Bray).

Technologically, there are two main methods of iron smelting: direct and indirect. The indirect and most efficient method has only been in use in Western Europe since the late medieval period and is characterized by high temperatures (1600° C to 2000° C) and the production of metal in liquid form. Earlier iron production was achieved using the direct method in which temperatures of around 1200°C are typical and iron is produced in the solid state. Direct smelting was employed in iron production on Exmoor during the period under consideration.

Smelting consists of two main processes; the chemical reduction of ore to metal and the formation and separation from the metal of a liquid slag containing the unwanted impurities from the ore. Close control of temperature and the gaseous atmosphere of the smelting environment are needed for these two processes to occur. This is achieved through the use of a furnace, consisting commonly of a clay cylinder within which smelting takes place. Direct smelting produces a 'bloom' of iron; a spongy mass of metal mixed with slag which is, of course, the main object of the process. However, large volumes of waste material are also generated. These are dominated by slag, but also include significant amounts of fired and vitrified fragments of clay derived from the furnace structure. These waste by-products are archaeologically important, firstly, because their presence, sometimes in large deposits, is often the most obvious indication of past smelting on a site and provides vital evidence for its character and history. Secondly, because scientific analysis can provide insights into the technology of the smelting operation that produced them.

Slag cake from
Clatworthy Reservoir,
weighing 17kg.
(© Lee Bray).

An iron bloom contains a significant proportion of slag and is not readily workable. Instead, it must be refined and this is achieved through the final stage of iron production; the process of bloomsmithing in which the bloom is heated and hammered, squeezing the slag out to leave a consolidated block, or billet of iron which can then be transformed into a useful iron object.

Following bloomsmithing, the completed billets would have been transported from the iron working site and through markets and other networks transformed into a range of objects. These markets would have varied through time, and the scale and complexity of the sites described below hints at how external factors influenced and drove the Exmoor iron industry. The objects produced (tantalisingly these artefacts are never present) range from a huge array of household objects, construction materials and tools, agricultural implements through to military hardware and weapons. From the Roman to the medieval period a world without iron was as inconceivable as the modern world is to us without plastics.

Section cut through one of the large waste deposits at Sherracombe Ford, clearly showing the depth of material accumulated (© Exmoor Iron Project).

Sites for the Visitor

This section of the guide contains descriptions of early iron production sites in the Exmoor region that are accessible or visible to the general public from a public right of way. They are presented starting from the western side of Exmoor and progressing towards the east.

When visiting these sites safety is the most vital concern. Exmoor's weather can be harsh and so suitable clothing should be worn and outdoor equipment carried. Also, mining operations have been undertaken on several of the sites discussed and these have left deep excavations. Extreme caution is advised especially if conditions underfoot are wet or slippery. You are also advised to carry a large scale Ordnance Survey map with you.

Much of Exmoor is privately owned, and access is permitted under various agreements. You should restrict yourself to public rights of way and agreed access land and are advised to check on the accessibility of these sites before visiting them. Please follow The Countryside Code.

See the map in the centre pages showing locations of all of the sites discussed.

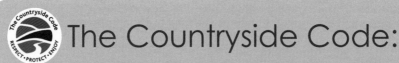

The Countryside Code:

- Be safe - plan ahead and follow any signs

- Leave gates and property as you find them

- Protect plants and animals, and take your litter home

- Keep dogs under close control

- Consider other people

Sherracombe Ford

NGR: SS 719 366

Status: On private land where there is no public access; visible from the adjoining public footpath.

Location: (plan on page 14) Sherracombe Ford can be reached from Brayford by following the road towards Simonsbath for 4km. At the Poltimore Arms (SS 724 356) turn left; the end of Sherracombe Lane (SS 725 357) leading to the site is on the left 100m further on. From Simonsbath, follow the road towards Brayford for approximately 4km to Kinsford Gate. Sherracombe Lane is the second turning on the right, approximately 2km further on.

Sherracombe Lane is a public right of way, but vehicular access is not advised. Instead park cars on the road at its eastern end and walk approximately 1km until Sherracombe Ford is reached.

Description

Sherracombe Ford is an iron smelting site situated below Five Barrows Hill in the steep-sided valley of a tributary stream of the River Bray, running in a south-westerly direction off the southern flank of Exmoor. Although there is no public access to the site, a good impression of its layout is easily gained as the earthworks are visible from the track which runs adjacent to its western end.

The iron working site at Sherracombe Ford is very well-preserved, having suffered little disruption since it was abandoned. As a result its archaeological features are readily identifiable. They are concentrated to the north of the stream - the focus of activity on the site - and comprise two main types. Most obvious are the large deposits of waste which are the by-product of iron smelting. Two deposits are visible as large, rounded dumps, approximately 2 to 3 metres high,

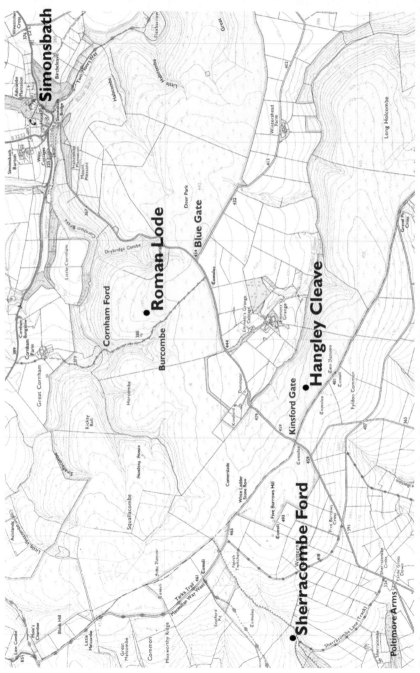

Map showing the locations of Sherracombe Ford, Hangley Cleave and Roman Lode.

protruding from the valley side. One of these is just inside the fence at the western end of the site. Natural weathering has eroded the dump's side exposing a loosely-packed mass of slag fragments. The second waste deposit, crowned by scrubby trees, can be seen from a higher vantage point further along the track to the west, at the eastern end of the site beside the stream.

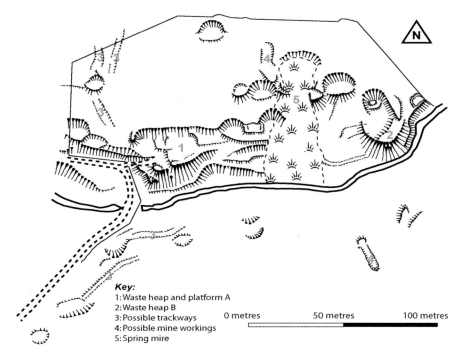

Key:
1: Waste heap and platform A
2: Waste heap B
3: Possible trackways
4: Possible mine workings
5: Spring mire

0 metres   50 metres   100 metres

Plan of Sherracombe Ford showing its major archaeological features
(© Exmoor National Park Authority).

The second types of features are flat platforms of varying sizes cut into the valley slopes. Large examples are positioned above each waste heap. They formed the main working areas of the site with the waste from the furnaces being dumped downhill, slowly forming the waste heaps which, over time, built out laterally from the valley side to create the features we see today. Also present are between ten and fifteen other platforms, not associated with waste deposits. These may have been used for iron ore roasting, charcoal storage, artefact production, or they may even have been for houses. Most are located on the northern side of the stream and two are located beside the track to the north-west of the gate. Several platforms are also located on the southern side of the stream and are easily visible in the field to the east of the track as it descends the slope to the valley bottom.

Other, more subtle, features are also present. For example, several platforms in the western part of the site are associated with well used former trackways. These platforms are also situated at a distance from the smelting operations and may have been for houses, but without excavation, this cannot be proved. Another trackway which was shown by excavation to be metalled with slag runs around the base of the western waste heap and heads towards the eastern one. It is likely that this represents the main route by which materials were transported across the site. Its location also suggests that the site was reached in the Roman period in much the same way as it is today: where the modern bridge crosses the stream.

Sherracombe Ford was investigated in detail by the Exmoor Iron Project between 2002 and 2005. Fieldwork focussed mainly on the western waste deposit and its associated platform. The story of the site here proved to be one of frequent modification with the platform being recut many times, removing evidence of previous activity in the process. Even so, the surviving evidence was complex, and included two well-preserved furnaces and a workshop in which iron blooms had been smithed over a significant period of time. Excavation through the waste deposit itself revealed a substantial sequence of dumped material reaching almost 3m thick. Around 500 sherds of pottery were recovered during the excavations, which suggest that the site was operating during the later 2nd century and first half of the 3rd century AD, a period during which the Roman Empire was at its height.

Excavated furnace setting at Sherracombe Ford. The orange coloured material has been discoloured by heat and marks the location of a furnace which was used and rebuilt many times (© Exmoor Iron Project).

Several thousand tonnes of smelting waste are present in heaps A and B (see plan on page 15). The excavated evidence suggests that this was generated by continuous smelting operations over the course of about 100 years, implying that production on the site was probably near-continuous and undertaken by specialist smelters. The character of the smelting waste deposits suggests that smelting was efficiently and expertly done with very little waste of materials. A bloomsmithing workshop implies that the raw blooms produced by smelting were refined to workable iron billets before leaving the site. The market for the iron billets from Sherracombe Ford is not known, but the intensity of production suggests that they were transported away from the locality to meet wider needs.

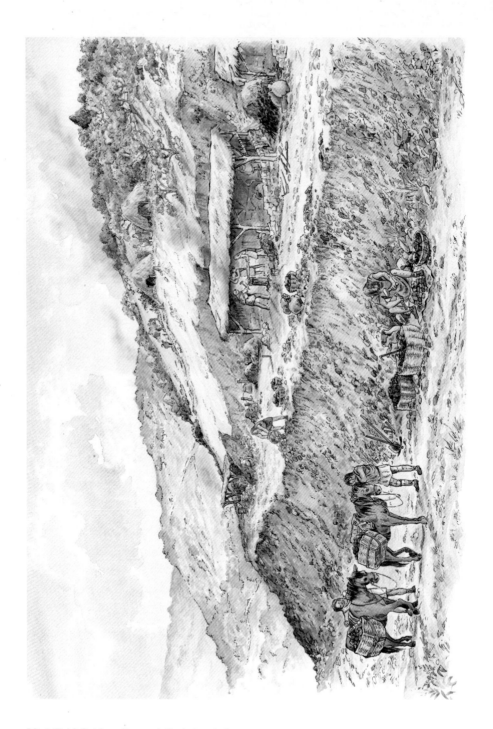

Left: Reconstruction of operations at Sherracombe Ford. A smelt has just been completed and the bloom is being consolidated in the building on the platform. Meanwhile the debris of the smelt is being dumped on the waste heap while, in the foreground, a load of ore is being delivered and ore-sorting is being undertaken (© Anne Leaver).

Above: Reconstruction of bloomsmithing at Sherracombe Ford. Here the bloom has just been extracted from the furnace and is undergoing initial consolidation in which two strikers, under the direction of the smith, are forcing slag from the bloom and compacting the metal while it is still soft and hot (© Anne Leaver).

Roman Lode

NGR: SS 753 382

Status: On public access land; owned by Exmoor National Park Authority

Location: (plan on page 14) From Simonsbath take the road south towards South Molton and continue for around 2km to the top of the hill at Blue Gate where very limited parking is available in a lay-by.

To reach Blue Gate from Brayford, follow the Simonsbath road for 3.5km and turn left at the Poltimore Arms junction and continue for approximately 4km.

From Blue Gate continue on foot 200m along the road to the entrance to the restricted byway, heading north-west across Burcombe towards Cornham Ford. Continue along this track for around 400m and, just before it begins to descend towards the Barle Valley, veer off right onto the moorland. The Roman Lode openwork is situated 300m from the track, the site of recent excavations being located at its eastern end.

Description

Roman Lode is the local name given to a long openwork running west-east for 500m across open moorland. It can be imagined that formerly – before mining began - it was a surface outcrop of a large iron ore deposit. Trial mining, during which several shafts were sunk along the lode, was undertaken here in the mid-19th century, although it never proved sufficiently profitable to be expanded and was abandoned after a few years. The shafts from these efforts are still visible today, although earlier workings dominate the site in the form of the massive openwork running the length of the ore body outcrop and reaching depths of around 5m and widths of 15m. Although continuous, the morphology of this openwork consists, in its deepest parts, of substantial pits linked by narrower sections. The implication is that the richer parts of the ore body were exploited by the pits before the remainder was extracted from the narrow trenches between. The date of these workings remains unknown although it is probable that they are responsible for the modern name of the site when Victorian miners ascribed earlier workings to the Romans or the 'Old Men'. It is unlikely that the visible openwork is entirely Roman although it is possible that some of the workings may have originated then.

Aerial view of the Roman Lode openwork (© English Heritage).

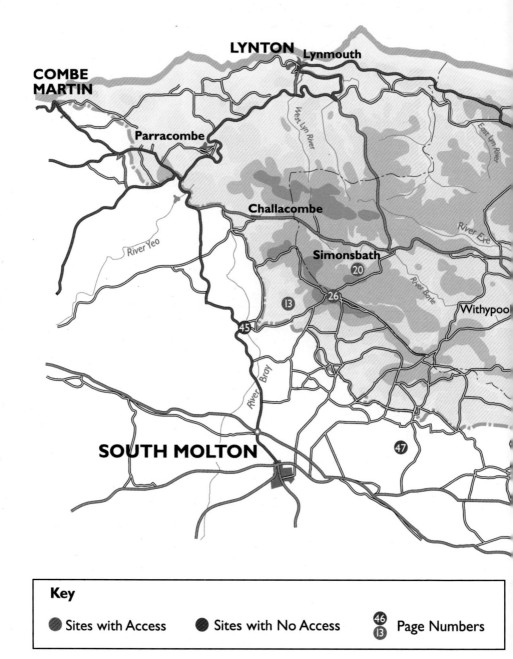

Map showing locations of the sites discussed.

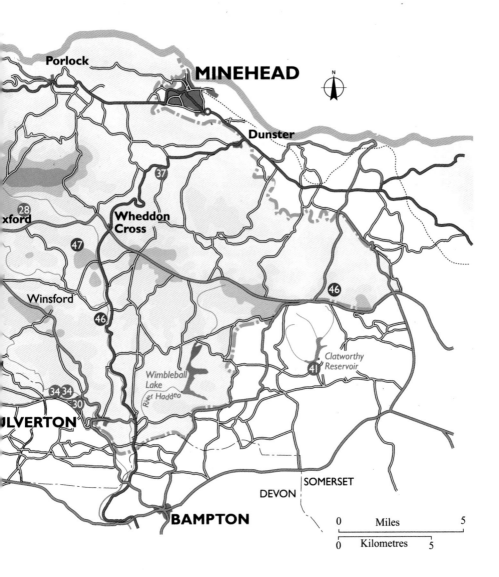

Porlock

MINEHEAD

N

Dunster

37

28
xford

**Wheddon
Cross**

47

Winsford

46

46

Clatworthy
Reservoir

Wimbleball
Lake

41

River Haddeo

34 34

30

JLVERTON

SOMERSET

DEVON

BAMPTON

0   Miles   5

0   Kilometres   5

© Copyright Exmoor National Park 2010

Ground view of the Roman Lode openwork (© R. Wilson-North).

Excavations at the eastern end of the openwork, between 2002 and 2004, by the Exmoor Iron Project, revealed a further period of mining, also undated, but perhaps even earlier than the openwork itself. The evidence for this took the form of a series of pits around 2m in diameter and perhaps 2 to 3m deep. In the same area was found the earliest evidence of people interacting with iron ore deposits. This consisted of a hearth dating to the Early Bronze Age (around1800 BC) and a deposit containing broken quartz fragments. The nature of this activity remains obscure; the hearth dates from a period at least 1000 years before iron metallurgy was adopted in Britain, but it does confirm that Roman Lode has been the focus of human activity for the last 4000 years. Possible interpretations focus around the possibility that quartz was being processed to yield copper ore within. However, much more work is needed at the site to place the ambiguous evidence so far found in a proper context.

Reconstruction of a potential mining scene at Roman Lode during the Roman period. It is a relatively small-scale operation involving a handful of people. In the foreground ore is being dug from a mining pit with flaring sides, shown in cutaway view, while in the background the ore is being processed, the waste being broken off and discarded. Later, the selected ore fragments will be transported to a smelting site where fuel is more readily available than on the high moorlands of Exmoor (© Anne Leaver).

Hangley Cleave

NGR: SS 745 365

Status: on public access land; private owner.

Location: (plan on page 14) Take the South Molton road south from Simonsbath continue for 4km, past Blue Gate until the Kinsford Gate crossroads is reached. Turn left here and park in the lay-by immediately on the left.

From Brayford, follow the Simonsbath road for 3km to the Poltimore Arms. Turn left at the junction here and continue for 2km to Kinsford Gate.

After parking, continue eastwards, following the road along the crest of the ridge for approximately 200m, until the first gate onto the moorland to the left is reached. The dumps of the mine workings are visible around 50m to the north.

Description

Hangley Cleave is an iron mining site on the Devon/Somerset border, around 2km south of Simonsbath. It consists of two intercutting linear openworks, each around 100m long. The earliest trends roughly east-west and has a morphology like the openwork at Roman Lode, suggesting that it was created through the linking of a series of pits dug along the linear outcrop of an iron lode. The date of this openwork is currently unknown, but the other, which trends approximately north-south, dates to the 19th century and is a good example of the prospecting practice of that period of using pre-existing mine workings as indicators of mineralization. Also in the 19th century a shaft was sunk towards the eastern end of the older openwork and an adit driven to intersect the mineral body from the north. The latter is located 250m to the north and, although now blocked, its distinctive linear spoil heap is still apparent.

Aerial view of the Hangley Cleave mine workings (© English Heritage).

Kitnor Heath

NGR: SS 873 396

Status: on public access land; private owner.

Location: (plan on page 29) From Exford, follow the B3224 eastwards towards Wheddon Cross for 2km and park in the layby at the side of the road. From this point (SS 875 392), a bridleway leaves the road heading northwards and, after 500m, leads to the mine workings.

Description

Kitnor Heath is another site where an outcropping iron ore deposit has been exploited in the past. The main features are three linear openworks, trending east-west, following the outcrop of the ore body for around 300m. There are also areas of dumping with different morphologies and several large pits, which are probably extraction features and are located between the westernmost and central openwork. The central and eastern openworks are fairly regular in shape, with steep, straight sides and flat bottoms, suggesting large-scale, methodical working and probably date to the 19th century. The western openwork differs in that its morphology is similar to that seen at Roman Lode and Hangley Cleave, giving the impression of a series of pits that have been linked together by further extraction. The presence of further pits, isolated from the openwork, supports this interpretation. It seems possible that the central and eastern openworks were originally of a similar character, but have been altered by 19th century prospecting or trial mining, producing their current form. The implication is that Kitnor Heath is a mining site at which the ore deposit has been exploited during many periods.

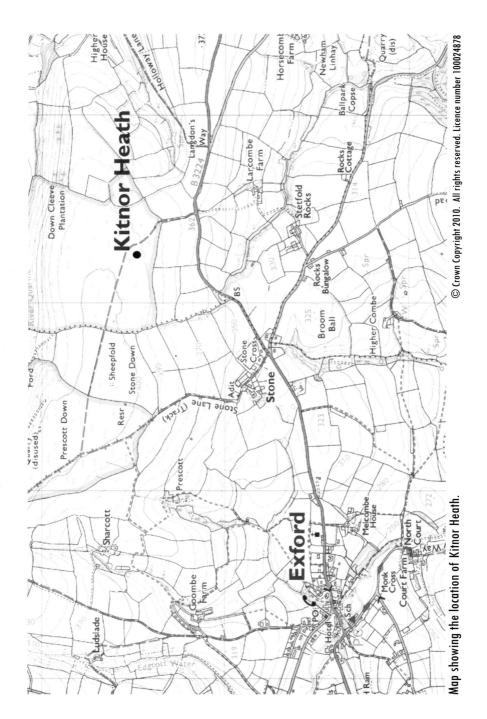

Map showing the location of Kitnor Heath.

Blacklake Wood

NGR: SS 904 287

Status: on private land, but visible from the adjacent road.

Location: (plan on page 31) From Dulverton town centre follow Northmoor Road northwards beside the River Barle. At a point around 1.5km from Dulverton, turn left just before the road turns sharply right and begins to climb out of the river valley. Shortly after the turning the road turns sharply to the left and crosses Marsh Bridge over the River Barle. Continue over the bridge, passing Kennel Farm on the left. Blacklake Wood is situated next to the hedge on the left, around 100m after the farm. Parking is very restricted so care should be taken and it must be emphasized that, although the site is visible, it is situated on private land and is not accessible to the public.

Description

Blacklake Wood is a smelting site situated on the southern side of the Barle Valley, 1km west of Dulverton. The major archaeological feature consists of an elongated smelting waste deposit around 30m long, 10m wide and up to 2m thick which is situated adjacent to the hedge and thus is readily visible from the road.

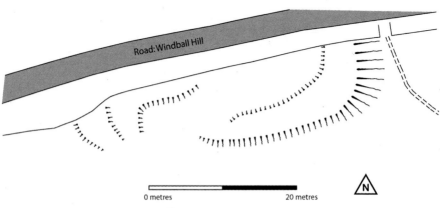

Earthwork plan of Blacklake Wood (© English Heritage).

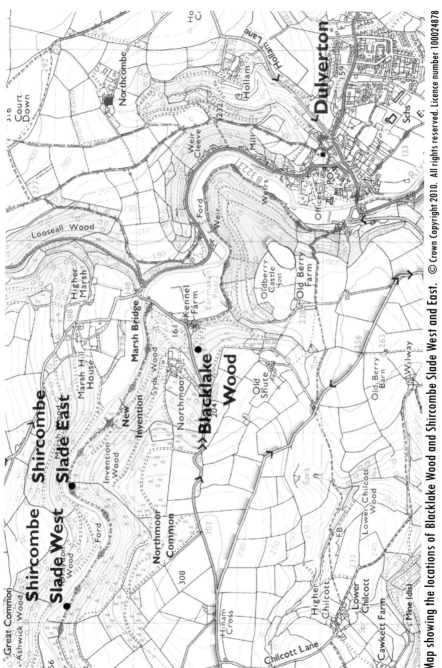

Map showing the locations of Blacklake Wood and Shircombe Slade West and East.

The waste heap at Blacklake Wood (© Exmoor Iron).

Excavations by the Exmoor Iron Project in 2005, revealed a thick sequence of smelting waste and the truncated remains of a furnace as well as ore roasting hearths. The very small ceramic assemblage and radiocarbon dating of charcoal recovered during the excavations suggested the site was active during the 3rd and 4th centuries; the later Roman period, somewhat later than the smelting at Sherracombe Ford.

The excavated evidence suggested a different style of production in comparison with Sherracombe Ford; activity on the site was perhaps more episodic, the use of resources such as ore and charcoal being less efficient and more wasteful, while the overall scale of production was less, generating waste deposits in the order of hundreds of tonnes in size. The implication is that the economic and perhaps social conditions in which iron production on Exmoor occurred had changed. Iron production at Blacklake Wood probably exceeded local demand, but external markets had shrunk or become less certain since their 2nd and 3rd century heyday represented by Clatworthy Reservoir and Sherracombe Ford.

Reconstruction of smelting activity at Blacklake Wood with a single furnace in operation
(© Anne Leaver).

Barle Valley

NGR: SS 900 292, SS 897 294, SS 891 294

Status: private woodland crossed by a public right of way

Location: (plan on page 31) From Dulverton town centre follow Northmoor Road northwards beside the River Barle. At a point around 1.5km from Dulverton, turn left just before the road turns sharply right and begins to climb out of the river valley. Around 50m after the turning, there is a small area on the left beside the river where parking is available. Proceed on foot across Marsh Bridge over the River Barle and from here turn right past the house onto the track following the southern bank of the river. The sites (see below) are all adjacent to this track although the first, in the private garden of New Invention House is not accessible to the public.

Description

The valley of the River Barle, to the west of Dulverton, in addition to the Roman period smelting site at Blacklake Wood, also contains three small sites of medieval date. One of these, at New Invention House (SS 900 292), is situated in a private garden and is not accessible to the public. Small scale excavation at New Invention House recovered ceramics dating to the 13th-15th centuries. The other two; Shircombe Slade East and Shircombe Slade West are located beside the public right of way that runs along the southern side of the Barle Valley from Marsh Bridge to Hawkridge.

The first of these, Shircombe Slade East, (SS 897 294) consists of two small heaps of smelting waste, 2 to 3m in diameter, situated adjacent to the track. Despite their initial appearance that they have been dumped there, small-scale excavation of the deposits has revealed that they are in situ. Radiocarbon dates obtained from charcoal recovered during this work yielded dates within the later medieval period.

Shircombe Slade West (SS 891 294) is situated around 500m west, at a point in the river valley where the flood plain widens on the southern side of the river. Although still not large, with perhaps just a few tens of tonnes of smelting waste, it is a little more substantial than both Shircombe Slade East and New Invention House. Three deposits of smelting waste are clearly visible on the flat surface of the flood plain as heaps up to 1m in height. Also apparent are the stone footings of three small buildings. Excavation by the Exmoor Iron Project revealed one of these to contain the stone-constructed base of a furnace, lined with clay and preserving, in situ, the last flow of slag from its final use. The function of the other two buildings remains unclear, although they may have served as storage areas or accommodation for the smelters. Pottery dated the activity here to the late medieval period.

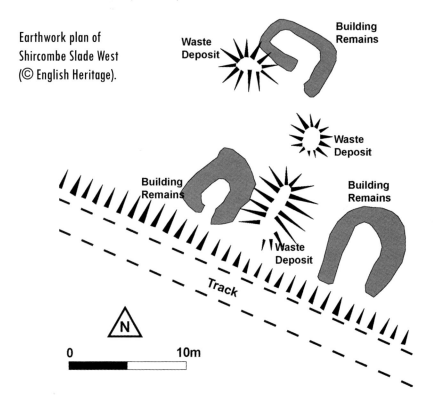

Earthwork plan of Shircombe Slade West (© English Heritage).

Left: Reconstruction drawing showing Shircombe Slade West during the medieval period. On the left, platforms have been cut into the hillside and are being used to make charcoal, while on the flat ground next to the river, rough buildings have been constructed to house iron smelting operations (© Anne Leaver).

Although all three of the Barle Valley sites are broadly contemporary, it is unlikely they were in operation at the same time. The small amounts of smelting waste present at each are suggestive of relatively short-lived activity lasting a few years at most and perhaps operating seasonally. The reasons for such potentially sporadic iron production are difficult to discern, but the apparently temporary nature of the sites implies that smelting was carried out to meet local needs at times when iron was not readily available from other sources. This is in stark contrast to the Roman-period production at Sherracombe Ford, Clatworthy Reservoir and even Blacklake Wood, where the scale and continuity of operations suggests a wider market for the iron.

Timberscombe Hillslope Enclosure

NGR: SS 957 414

Status: public access land; owned by Exmoor National Park Authority

Location: (plan on page 38) From Timberscombe Church, follow the minor road south for approximately 1km until, as the road climbs a steep, wooded hill, it turns sharply to the right. Shortly after this, on the right, is the entrance to the track to the site. Restricted parking is available on the left side of the road 50m past the track.

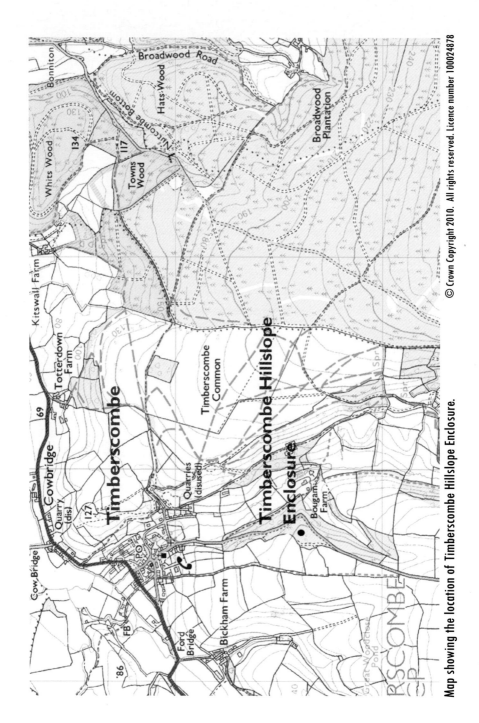

Map showing the location of Timberscombe Hillslope Enclosure.

Description

This site is a fine example of an Iron Age settlement, usually described as a hillslope enclosure. It is roughly rectangular, bounded by an earthwork bank and ditch. Such sites were relatively common in the Iron Age and Roman period in the Exmoor region, and in the South-West generally. They are most often interpreted as farmsteads probably occupied by extended families. The bank and ditch enclose an area of approximately 0.5 hectares situated on a bluff, and the site uses the steep terrain to the north to enhance the appearance of the rampart. Iron smelting slag has been recovered from the surface during field visits, and geophysical and geochemical surveys have detected possible metal working. It seems likely that the enclosed settlement at Timbersombe was producing iron. If this activity is Iron Age then the site contains some of the earliest evidence for iron production in the Exmoor region.

Aerial view of Timberscombe Hillslope Enclosure (© English Heritage).

Reconstruction of Timberscombe Hillslope Enclosure during its occupation (© Jane Brayne).

Clatworthy Reservoir

NGR: ST 035 305

Status: owned by Wessex Water, but accessible to the public.

Location: (plan on page 42) From Ralegh's Cross (ST 039 344), proceed eastwards on the B3224. Continue for approximately 1km and take the first turning on the right towards Wiveliscombe. After 2km turn first right to Clatworthy, turning right at the junction in the village. Follow the lane for around 1km until the entrance to Clatworthy Reservoir is reached on the right, where there is parking and a picnic area.

From Bampton, take the B3190 northwards towards Watchet, continuing for approximately 10 km, through Morebath until Upton is reached. From Upton continue along the B3190 for 2km to Sperry Cross and turn right towards Wiveliscombe. Take the first turning on the left after a kilometre and continue down the lane for a similar distance until the entrance to Clatworthy Reservoir is reached on the left after a sharp bend.

After parking, proceed on foot to the west and south, heading away from the dam and downhill towards the reservoir shore and the fishing lodge, which marks the known eastern edge of the site. To explore further follow the track along the southern shore of the reservoir.

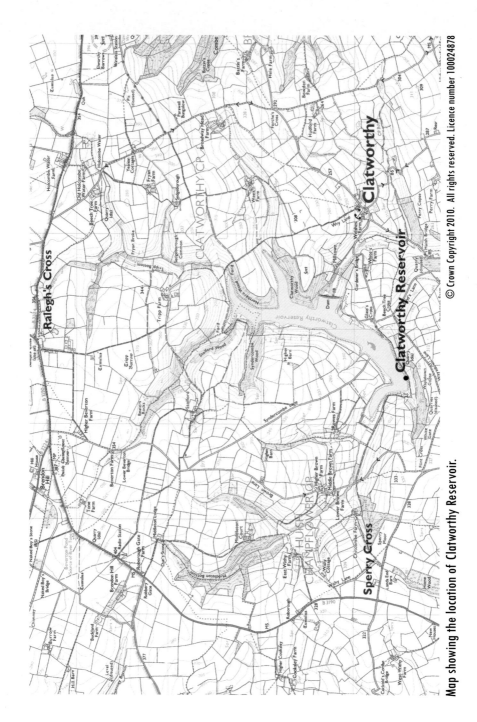

Map showing the location of Clatworthy Reservoir.

Description

Clatworthy Reservoir was constructed in the late 1950s by damming the headwaters of the River Tone. In the process, a tributary valley, known as Sindercombe, leading off to the south, was also flooded, forming one arm of the reservoir. This name appears in the Domesday Book as Syndercoma and is suggestive; the synder- element deriving from the Anglo-Saxon word, sinder, meaning slag. The implication that deposits of this material were known here at least as far back as the 11th century, and probably before, was confirmed during the construction of the reservoir when smelting waste deposits associated with Romano-British pottery were uncovered.

Recent field survey has revealed six deposits of smelting waste distributed along 500m of the southern shoreline of the reservoir. In most cases these are not obvious; only deposit C is visible as a pronounced hummock just above the reservoir shoreline, although some slag fragments are present in the track bed above deposit D. The waste deposits become more readily apparent when the water level of the reservoir falls, as the beach below each is littered with fragments of slag and other material including, iron ore, quartz,

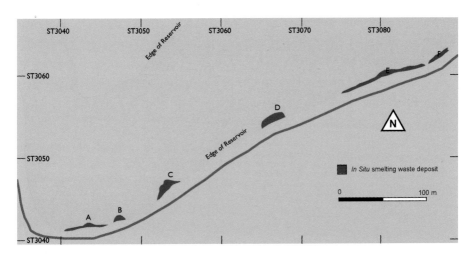

Plan showing the main archaeological features at Clatworthy Reservoir (© Lee Bray).

furnace debris and pottery. The source of the ore smelted on the site is currently unknown. Field survey revealed no sign of mineralization in its immediate vicinity and it seems likely that ore was obtained from the Brendon Hill deposits a few kilometres to the north where openworks are present on a number of sites.

Small-scale excavations were undertaken at Clatworthy Reservoir, in 2005, into waste deposit C, which confirmed that it was undisturbed and of Roman date. Interestingly, among the finds of this work was a fragment of window glass which, when added to a probable hypocaust tile fragment recovered during previous field survey, suggests the presence of a substantial building constructed using Roman building techniques, somewhere in the immediate vicinity. The nature of this building and its precise location are unknown. Excavated finds, including a sherd of a glass drinking vessel, suggest that the site dates from the early 2nd century, or perhaps late 1st century and continues into the late 2nd century.

The total amount of smelting waste on the site is probably in the order of thousands of tonnes, suggesting a smelting operation on a substantial scale, which, according to the excavated evidence, operated continuously for several generations. This style and scale of operation probably suggests specialist production of iron for markets significantly larger than those available locally. The recovery of glass drinking vessels, amphorae used for shipping olive oil from southern Spain and the presence of a substantial building with a hypocaust system and glazed windows, all suggest a degree of affluence among those running the site.

Additional Sites

This section comprises a list and brief description of other iron production sites; they are presented in alphabetical order. All of these sites are on private land and are not accessible; they are presented here for completeness in order to provide a fuller picture of early iron production in the Exmoor region.

Brayford

NGR: SS 685 347

Description

The village of Brayford is situated on the south-western fringes of Exmoor, around 3km south-west of Sherracombe Ford. It is potentially the largest iron smelting site in the Exmoor region as fragments of debris have been recovered from many locations within the modern settlement. However, the very presence of the existing settlement means that it is difficult to understand and define the extent and nature of industrial activity there. What is known has come to light through accidental finds and material recovered largely by development-led excavation. The best evidence is derived from excavations undertaken in advance of development at the western end of the village around Bray Vale. These uncovered an in situ smelting waste heap of significant size. Although its full extent could not be determined, it may originally have been comparable in size with those at Sherracombe Ford. Further excavations in the area revealed parts of a working area containing the remains of a possible ore-roasting operation. This work also yielded an assemblage of over 2000 sherds of pottery, the largest of Roman date from North Devon, which suggests that smelting was contemporary with that at Sherracombe Ford, although it may have been longer-lived, perhaps lasting into the 4th century. This evidence, combined with other fragments from the rest of the village, suggests that Brayford was a centre of significant smelting activity in the past and that most of it dates to the Roman period.

Bridgetown

NGR: SS 924 332

Description

Little is known about iron exploitation in the past at Bridgetown, but smelting slag has been recovered from the western side of the valley of the river Exe during field visits, while an iron bloom was discovered during ploughing in the 19th century. It is likely that more intensive archaeological survey would reveal more information.

Colton Pits

NGR: ST 058 347

Description

This impressive iron mining site, although known, was, until recent years, concealed by a conifer plantation. It consists of a dense group of large pits up to 10m in diameter and 5m deep located on the surface outcrop of an iron body. This ore deposit was exploited during the 19th century by underground methods which encountered earlier subsurface workings. These, as with the substantial surface pits, are of unknown date, but it is possible especially in the case of the latter, that multiple phases of activity, potentially over a significant period, have occurred on the site.

Ison/Oldrey

NGR: SS 905 371

Description

This area contains prominent remains of iron exploitation from several periods. Most recent are 19th century shafts along the surface outcrop of an east-west trending iron ore deposit. The same lode is also followed by numerous pits, some comparable in size with those at Colton Pits, which are of an earlier, though unknown date. Some of the mining remains are likely to be medieval because a disturbed smelting site was excavated in 2005 in a private garden near Oldrey Farm, from which radiocarbon dates of this period were obtained.